Pocket M

The *Pocket Mentor* Series offers immediate solutions to common challenges managers face on the job every day. Each book in the series is packed with handy tools, self-tests, and real-life examples to help you identify your strengths and weaknesses and hone critical skills. Whether you're at your desk, in a meeting, or on the road, these portable guides enable you to tackle the daily demands of your work with greater speed, savvy, and effectiveness.

Books in the series:

Thinking Strategically

Expert Solutions to Everyday Challenges

Harvard Business Press

Boston, Massachusetts

Copyright 2010 Harvard Business School Publishing
All rights reserved
Printed in the United States of America
10 9 8 7

No part of this publication may be reproduced, stored in or introduced into a
retrieval system, or transmitted, in any form, or by any means (electronic,
mechanical, photocopying, recording, or otherwise), without the prior permission
of the publisher. Requests for permission should be directed to permissions@hbsp.
harvard.edu, or mailed to Permissions, Harvard Business School Publishing,
60 Harvard Way, Boston, Massachusetts 02163.

Library of Congress Cataloging-in-Publication Data

Thinking strategically : expert solutions to everyday challenges.
    p. cm. — (Pocket mentor series)
Includes bibliographical references.
ISBN 978-1-4221-2971-5 (pbk. : alk. paper)   1. Strategic planning.
2. Leadership.   I. Harvard Business School.
    HD30.28. T456 2010
    658.4'012—dc22

                                    2009051085

The paper used in this publication meets the requirements of the American National
Standard for Permanence of Paper for Publications and Documents in Libraries and
Archives Z39.48-1992.

Contents

Tips and Tools

Mentor's Message: Why Learn to Think Strategically?

As a manager, you work in one part of an organization that has many parts. And every day, you make decisions—choices that can help or hurt your organization, depending on how strategic they are. To make decisions that generate the best possible results overall for your organization, you need to consider the wider implications of each course of action you're considering. And you have to work around the fact that you'll always have limited (and often confusing) information with which to approach complex decisions.

To make the wisest possible choices, you need to *think strategically*. But thinking strategically is a process consisting of a set of skills that you must practice, learn, and apply in a particular sequence. This book helps you master the skills essential to the process. You'll start by discovering how to understand the business environment you're operating in and how to clarify objectives you want to achieve—to set the stage for making a strategic decision. Next, you'll learn how to apply five crucial strategic thinking skills: identifying relationships, patterns, and trends in your business environment; thinking creatively; analyzing information; prioritizing your actions;

and making the trade-offs that inevitably come with choosing one course of action.

Master the strategic thinking process and its specific skills, and you become a true strategic partner in your organization.

David J. Collis, Mentor

David J. Collis is a professor in the strategy unit at the Harvard Business School, where he teaches in the MBA and Executive Education programs. He is an expert on corporate strategy and global competition, and is the author of the recent books *Corporate Strategy* (with Cynthia Montgomery) and *Corporate Headquarters* (with Michael Goold and David Young). His work has been frequently published in *Harvard Business Review*, *Academy of Management Journal*, *Strategic Management Journal*, *European Management Journal*, and in many books, including *Managing the Multibusiness Company*, *International Competitiveness*, and *Beyond Free Trade*. In 2008, Professor Collis won the 50th Anniversary McKinsey award for the best article published in *Harvard Business Review* in that year.

In addition to teaching, Professor Collis consults to several major U.S. corporations, and serves on the board of trustees of the Hult International Business School, and the advisory boards of Vivaldi Partners and Folderwave. He is also the cofounder of the eLearning company E-Edge, and of the advisory firm Ludlow Partners.

Thinking Strategically: The Basics

An Overview of Thinking Strategically

Your boss just told you to "think strategically"—but what does *that* mean? In the pages that follow, we'll take a closer look at several key aspects of thinking strategically—what it is, why it's important, who needs to think strategically, what distinguishes strategic thinkers, and what are the steps in the strategic thinking process.

What is strategic thinking?

In its most basic sense, strategic thinking is about analyzing opportunities and problems from a broad perspective and understanding the potential impact your actions might have on others. Strategic thinkers visualize what might or could be, and take a holistic approach to day-to-day issues and challenges. And they make this an ongoing process rather than a onetime event.

Like other managers, you routinely encounter complex situations, difficult problems, and challenging decisions. Your job is to deal with these situations as best you can by using the information you have. In an ideal world, you would have access to all the information you need to navigate through these challenges. Unavoidably, however, you have only a limited amount of information to work with. And because you sit in a particular part of your organization, you have a limited view of the forces that lie outside your sphere of influence.

Strategic thinking helps you overcome these limitations. When you think strategically, you lift your head above your day-to-day work and consider the larger environment in which you're operating. You ask questions and challenge assumptions about how things work in your company and industry. You gather complex, sometimes ambiguous data and interpret it. And you use the insights gained to make smart choices and select appropriate courses of action.

Moreover, you do all these things with an eye toward generating the best possible business results tomorrow, using the opportunities presented to you today.

Why is strategic thinking important?

When you and others in your organization think strategically, you generate important benefits for your organization:

- You chart a course for your group that aligns with the overall corporate strategy.

- You make smart long-term decisions that complement and align with decisions that others in your organization are making.

- You gain your employees' commitment to supporting your decisions.

- You boost your group's performance and maximize business results.

- You foster a culture that supports fresh thinking and embraces strategic initiative.

Strategic thinking also nets you valuable professional and personal benefits—including the respect and appreciation of your supervisor, peers, and direct reports.

The real voyage of discovery consists not in seeking new lands but in seeing with new eyes.
—Marcel Proust

Who needs to think strategically?

In today's highly competitive and fast-changing business world, *everyone* in an organization must know how to think strategically. Only then can an organization leverage the full range of creativity and knowledge embodied throughout its workforce.

Strategic thinking can be especially effective when it's done collaboratively as well as individually. By thinking strategically in groups, you gain other people's perspectives on critical and complex issues—an important benefit in today's challenging business landscape.

Every manager in your organization has a unique view of how the company operates. By asking peer managers questions about how they interact with people from various parts of the enterprise, you strengthen your understanding of how your actions might affect them and their work.

For instance, suppose you work in accounts receivable and want to overhaul your billing system. You know that the IT group, as well as all managers who generate bills, will be affected. However, you decide to ask others in the organization about how changing the billing system might have an impact on them. Through conversations with people in the marketing department, you learn that your proposed changes will have significant consequences for the package design group. Why? All designs will now need to incorporate a larger bar code to accommodate changes in the billing-system technology.

By collaborating with others, you gain greater insight into the complex ramifications of even seemingly minor decisions. This insight, in turn, helps you make more strategic choices.

What are the distinguishing characteristics of strategic thinkers?

Managers who think strategically demonstrate specific personal traits, behaviors, attitudes, and thinking skills. For example, you're on your way to becoming a strategic thinker if you exhibit the following *personal traits*:

- **Curiosity.** You're genuinely interested in what's going on in your unit, company, industry, and wider business environment.

- **Flexibility.** You're able to adapt approaches and shift ideas when new information suggests the need to do so.

- **Future focus.** You constantly consider how the conditions in which your group and company operate may change in the coming months and years. And you keep an eye out for opportunities that may prove valuable in the future—as well as threats that may be looming.

- **Positive outlook.** You view challenges as opportunities, and you believe that success is possible.

- **Openness.** You welcome new ideas from supervisors, peers, employees, and outside stakeholders such as customers, suppliers, and business partners. You also take criticism well by not reacting in a defensive manner.

- **Breadth.** You continually work to broaden your knowledge and experience, so you can see connections and patterns across seemingly unrelated fields of knowledge.

You have the makings of a strategic thinker if you continually anticipate your actions' impact on a wide range of individuals—including, but not limited to, your boss, direct reports, peers, and customers. To do this, you need to demonstrate the following *behaviors*:

- Seek other people's opinions.

- Ask questions and challenge assumptions about how the world works.

- Focus on the future.

- Identify the forces driving your unit's and company's performance and think about how to improve that performance.

- Watch the competition.

- Reassess who your customers are and what they value.

- Stay up to date on developments occurring in your unit, in other groups in the company, and in your industry overall.

- Open yourself to ongoing learning by reading books, magazines, and industry reports; attending seminars; and talking with experts.

By practicing these behaviors, you more readily spot valuable new opportunities to capitalize on. And you identify and repel potential threats before they can do any real damage.

Finally, strategic thinkers demonstrate characteristic *thinking skills*. They:

- Objectively analyze a situation and evaluate the pros, cons, and implications of any course of action.

- Grasp abstract ideas and put the "pieces" together to form a coherent picture.

- Generate a wide range of options, visualize new possibilities, and formulate fresh approaches to their work.

- Factor hunches into their decision making without allowing their hunches to dominate the final outcome.

- Understand the cause-and-effect linkages among the many elements that make up a system—whether the system is their team, unit, or organization, or a project or process.

In strategy it is important to see distant things as if they were close and to take a distanced view of close things.
—Miyamoto Musashi

What are the steps in strategic thinking?

Strategic thinking can be broken down into two phases, each of which consists of specific steps.

Phase 1—setting the stage—consists of two steps:

1. **Seeing the big picture**—understanding the broader business environment in which you operate.

2. **Articulating strategic objectives**—determining what you hope to achieve by thinking strategically.

Phase 2—applying your skills—consists of five additional steps:

3. **Identifying relationships, patterns, and trends**—spotting patterns across seemingly unrelated events, and categorizing related information to reduce the number of issues you must grapple with at one time.

4. **Getting creative**—generating alternatives, visualizing new possibilities, challenging your assumptions, and opening yourself to new information.

5. **Analyzing information**—sorting out and prioritizing the most important information while making a decision, managing a project, handling a conflict, and so forth.

6. **Prioritizing your actions**—staying focused on your objectives while handling multiple demands and competing priorities.

7. **Making trade-offs**—recognizing the potential advantages and disadvantages of an idea or course of action, making choices regarding what you will and won't do, and balancing short- and long-term concerns

In the remaining sections of this book, we'll take a closer look at each of these steps.

Step 1: See the Big Picture

trategic thinkers continually improve their view of the larger "business ecosystem" in which they operate. They understand their company's and unit's strategies. They stay up to date on the issues and concerns of their customers, competitors, and industry as they relate to their job function. And they consider the potential impact of their decisions and actions on the company overall and on their boss, managers of other units and teams, and employees. They do all this with a long-term perspective rather than focusing only on the short-term implications of their actions. They then use their awareness of the big picture to inform their on-the-job choices.

Understanding company and unit strategies

Awareness of your company's and unit's strategies is vital to your ability to think strategically. Do whatever it takes to understand the corporate strategy and how it affects your unit's strategy. Talk with your boss and peer managers, examine annual reports and other company publications, and listen to your CEO's speeches.

Sometimes the way in which executives allocate resources in your company can suggest something about the high-level strategy. If you observe the company is investing in acquisitions of competing firms, you might deduce that its strategy involves eradicating rivals and growing its market share.

Then use your understanding of this strategy to ensure that your group supports it. For example, suppose your company has a clearly

?What Would YOU Do?

Toying with New Ideas

S HANE IS A PRODUCT MANAGER at Bailey Toys and Games. Top management has recently challenged all units to increase revenues by 5 percent in the coming year. Shane's boss has asked him to think strategically about ways to fulfill this mandate.

Shane has some ideas about how to update some of the games in his product line with new packaging and new features that would really appeal to customers. He'd like to explore the implications and feasibility of his ideas, but he's not sure how to proceed.

What would YOU do? The mentor will suggest a solution in *What You COULD Do.*

---

stated strategy of expanding into new markets overseas. You can use awareness of this high-level strategy to define your group's direction.

- If you lead a product development group, you might evaluate the appeal that your existing products have in the targeted overseas market.

- If you lead a market research group, you may want to design surveys and other tools for testing potential interest in your company's offerings in the intended new market.

- If you lead a customer service group, perhaps you'll explore how your group's services can be scaled to meet the demand of the overseas customer segment you'll be serving.

With every important decision that you weigh, ask, "Will what I'm considering doing help my unit and company carry out its strategy? Or will my proposed course of action make it more difficult for us to achieve our strategic goals?" "Steps for understanding your company's and unit's strategies" provides additional guidance for this aspect of seeing the big picture.

Steps for understanding your company's and unit's strategies

1. **Determine whether your company and unit have strategic plans.** Ask your boss whether strategic plans exist at the corporate and unit levels. If so, see if you can obtain copies. The information contained within these documents will help you gain a better understanding of your company's and unit's strategic missions, visions, and goals.

2. **Talk with your boss about your corporate and unit strategies.** After you have reviewed all the strategy documents that are available to you, talk with your boss about the company's and unit's future direction. Ask your boss to tell you about corporate or unit planning sessions that he or she has attended.

3. **Ask for your peers' perspectives on company and unit strategies.** Talk with other managers in your organization to understand how the company and units approach strategy formulation, planning, and execution.

4. **Observe the decisions and messages that executives and managers in your organization are communicating.** Read or listen to presentations that the CEO has made to the board, investors, and others. CEO presentations typically communicate direction and progress toward both short-term business goals and long-term strategic initiatives. Also:
   - If your company is public, read its annual report.
   - Review your organization's Web site.
   - Review your company's advertisements and press releases.
   - Look at marketing and product information.
   - Examine newsletters and other communication channels for information about your organization's strategy.
   - Attend all company meetings in which strategies and re-sults are discussed. Doing so will keep you on top of changes taking place in the organization.

5. **Be able to discuss your company's and unit's strategies with others.** By talking about your corporate and unit strategies and answering questions that others may have, you will deepen your understanding of the strategies at play within your organiza-tion. Questions you should be able to answer include:
   - What are your company's and unit's strategies?
   - Why were they chosen?
   - What is needed for the strategies to succeed?

Analyzing customers, competitors, and your industry

When thinking strategically, you need to consider what's going on outside your company as well as what's going on inside. That means staying current with external customers' needs, competitors' moves, and industry trends. Your job function will determine how much you'll need to make this a priority.

For example, if you work in sales, you'll need to know your customers, competition, and industry intimately. If you work in manufacturing, however, you may not need to study your company's competition quite as closely.

The future influences the present just as much as the past.
—Friedrich Nietzsche

To assess developments outside your company, ask these questions:

- **Customers.** "Who are our customers, and what do they value? How might their needs evolve in the future?" Customer surveys, focus groups, and other methods can help you gain answers to these questions. For example, after surveying customers about their latest challenges, one manager at an industrial-gas supplier proposed that the company start providing environmental consulting services to customers. He won approval for his idea, and the new service proved a hit—enabling the gas supplier to capture more of its customers' spending.

- **Competitors.** "Who are our current competitors, and what tactics are they using? How are we different from them?

What strengths do they have that might prove a threat to us? What weaknesses might they have that we could exploit?" You can gain information about competing companies by becoming their customer yourself, reading analysts' reports (of publicly traded companies), and networking with other professionals who are familiar with these firms.

For instance, one manager at a local retail store visited a major rival discount store in town and listened in on shoppers' conversations. He concluded that shoppers cared far more about the discounter's low prices than brand-name styles. The manager suggested to his store's executives that, to compete against the big discounter, they could strive to attract style-conscious customers. By going after a different customer segment than that sought by their rival, the store maintained a solid position in the business.

- **Industry.** "What trends—in technology, governmental policy, natural resources, and other key forces shaping our industry—might have important implications for our business?" You can stay on top of this information through reading a wide range of business publications, talking with other informed professionals, and participating in trade and professional associations.

  For example, while reading a food-industry trade journal, one manager learned that the government was considering requiring food companies to list additional ingredients in their product labeling. The manager knew if this legislation passed, the label size would increase and could potentially overlap with some of the marketing copy on the products. Thus, the manager met with people in the marketing department and together developed a solution that met everyone's needs. By having ideas ready, he was able to prepare his company for immediate compliance with the new legislation—should it pass—with minimal delay and disruption to the business.

Tip: Look at your group through your customers' and competitors' eyes. Ask, "What would I think of my group if I were a customer? A competitor? What would I see as my group's strengths and weaknesses?"

Considering internal stakeholders' priorities

Also take into account how your choices and ideas will affect the people around you in your organization—your supervisor, managers of other units and teams, and your direct reports. All these people are internal stakeholders in any important decision you make. Some may have an interest in the decision's outcome. Others will be profoundly affected by that outcome. Still others may want to block your plans or even oppose your course of action outright. Whatever the case, you'll need their support to implement your decisions.

The following approaches can help you systematically consider your internal stakeholders' needs and concerns:

- **Identify potential stakeholders and their interests.** When you're considering a course of action or a decision, brainstorm all the individuals who may be affected by or have an interest in your choice. Consider the business process that your decision will affect. Ask: "Who's involved in this business process? What are their roles and responsibilities? What's the nature of the relationships among them? What are their goals?"

- **Gather information from stakeholders.** Present your ideas to the stakeholders you've identified, and invite these individuals to share any concerns and ideas they might have. Ask open-ended questions about your idea, such as "What problems do you foresee? What ideas do you have for improving the plan? What's needed for this idea to work for you? What do you see as the pitfalls?"

- **Listen carefully to underlying issues.** Define problems from the perspective of each stakeholder, listening carefully to his or her concerns. Look for ways to address concerns that overlap multiple stakeholder groups.

For example, suppose you advocate adopting a new customer database to better manage customer relationships. This idea may raise concerns for several stakeholders: The IT group will need to spend extra time researching and installing the database. Your employees will have to learn how to use the new system. The finance group may be concerned about its cost. Managers in other units may not want to take the time to input customer data from their records. As time seems to be a common concern, you might propose a short pilot project that enables everyone to test the new database quickly before deciding whether to commit resources to a larger initiative.

Tip: Think "What if?" With every idea or course of action under consideration, ask yourself and others, "If we implement this idea, how will other units and stakeholders be affected? What might be the long-term ramifications of this decision?"

If you neglect to understand your internal stakeholders' concerns, you can inadvertently create widespread problems. For instance, suppose you run a manufacturing group at your organization. You decide to buy a piece of equipment that lets you produce five thousand units of a particular product part that your group manufactures, at a dramatically lower cost per unit. That's good news for your group's performance—but you discover that the decision has created problems for the key accounts group. Why? They've promised small, cost-effective, quick-delivery customized products for major customers. The set-up cost associated with switching the equipment for small runs is high in relation to the number of units being produced. Furthermore, to fulfill those orders, you have to wait until your new machine has finished a five thousand-unit run before you can use it to produce the smaller, customized orders. The expensive set-up fees and the delays in switching the equipment make it difficult for the key accounts group to promote customized orders and promptly fulfill those orders.

Use the "Worksheet for Seeing the Big Picture," located in the Tips and Tools section, to document your thoughts about each aspect of this step in thinking strategically.

What You COULD Do.

Remember Shane's question about how to explore ideas for enhancing his products to meet company goals?

Here's what the mentor suggests:

Shane realizes that many of the games in his product line require strategic thinking. He could use the same strategic thinking process to assess his ideas' potential and select an appropriate course of action. To do that, Shane would need to gain a solid understanding of the broader business environment in which he is operating and consider how his ideas would affect other parts of his organization. Then Shane could apply some strategic thinking skills, such as weighing the possible trade-offs of spending resources on repackaging existing products instead of developing new games. He could also engage his team in creative thinking sessions to generate other alternatives for increasing revenues and meeting the company's strategic goals.

Step 2: Articulate Strategic Objectives

Once you've gained a sense of the big picture, it's time to clarify your strategic objectives. That is, you need to determine what you hope to achieve through strategic thinking. Your boss, you, and the projects you think could generate strategic value can be important sources of information on objectives. Once you have some ideas for objectives, it's important to articulate them effectively—through a set of criteria called "SMART."

Understanding your boss's objectives

Often, your boss may define strategic objectives for you—for example, "We need to cut costs to improve company profitability." But if such objectives are presented in vague or overly general language, confusion may result. For instance, you might think you're satisfying the cost-cutting mandate by reducing expenses in your immediate group—only to discover that your boss wanted to implement broader-scale programs to cut costs across the entire division.

> *What do you want to achieve or avoid? The answers to this question are objectives. How will you go about achieving your desired results? The answer to this you can call strategy.*
> —William E. Rothschild

To avoid such misunderstandings, ask your boss questions about the objectives he or she defines for you. Examples might include:

- Where in our organization do we need to focus our cost-cutting efforts?

- What degree of cost cutting are we aiming for?

- Which processes am I free to change in order to cut costs, and which processes must remain untouched?

Also offer additional ideas about objectives your boss has defined. For instance, "Are there different objectives that can help us further enhance the company's profitability—such as boosting sales in addition to cutting costs? If we cut costs in this particular area, would these changes affect other areas of the company in ways that could ultimately raise costs and defeat our purpose?"

Taking a broader perspective and asking questions about how your potential actions will affect others are hallmarks of strategic thinking.

Tip: Don't assume you understand objectives mandated by your boss. Ask questions to gain the most specific possible understanding of what your boss wants you to achieve. Then augment your boss's ideas. Offer ideas for additional objectives that might generate valuable strategic results for your group and company.

Defining your own objectives

In addition to handling immediate objectives presented by your boss, you also need to define your own long-term objectives for your group. To do that, make time to regularly ask yourself questions such as the following:

- What should my group be doing in five years to make the best possible contribution to the company?

- What business will our organization be in five or ten years from now, and how can my group support that business?

- What changes might be looming on the business horizon, and how can my group best plan for and benefit from those changes?

By regularly asking such questions and gaining agreement from your boss on the strategic objectives for your group, you help ensure that your group stays on track and remains aligned with corporate strategy.

Tip: Envision future challenges for your group. Decide what your group needs to accomplish now in order to address challenges or take advantage of opportunities that may present themselves in the future.

Identifying project-related objectives

Frequently, you may come up with ideas for projects that you believe will generate important strategic value for your organization. For example, suppose you're a manager in the IT department and you propose developing a new database that will enable the company to acquire and analyze more comprehensive and accurate information about customers' preferences and purchasing activities. In your mind, the project's objective is clear: to improve knowledge of customer preferences so as to serve them more profitably. But other managers may have additional objectives in mind for the project—such as extracting customer information more quickly than before, obtaining customer reports in new formats, and so forth. If you try to satisfy all these objectives, the project scope may soon balloon to impossible proportions. Result? Resources end up getting spread too thin, and the project fails.

To think strategically in such situations, you need to clarify the strategic priority that the project is intended to serve. Here are some questions that can help you ensure that your project supports strategic objectives and balances the needs of various stakeholders with higher-level strategy:

- What is the perceived strategic need that this project is intended to satisfy?

- Who has a stake in the solution or outcome?

- How do the various stakeholders' goals for the project differ? Do their goals align with the higher-level strategic goals we're trying to achieve through this project?

- Are there other projects that would help us better satisfy the strategic need we've identified? If so, what are they? And how do they compare with the current proposed project—in terms of cost, feasibility, and so forth?

Tip: Define the project's purpose. Be able to articulate exactly how it will benefit your company. Avoid "scope creep," whereby you agree to expand the purpose of the project to accommodate a wide variety of demands from numerous stakeholders.

Making your objectives "SMART"

Whether your objectives have been given to you by your boss or you're creating your own objectives, make sure they are SMART—specific, measurable, achievable, realistic, and time bound. For example, one human resource task force charged with developing a new health care benefits plan defined the following SMART objective: "To recommend at the June board of directors' meeting the three providers that offer the best and broadest coverage at a cost that is at least 10 percent less than the company's current per-employee contribution." The table, "SMART objective and criteria," shows how this objective meets all five SMART criteria.

Use the "Worksheet for Clarifying Strategic Objectives," located in the Tips and Tools section, to document your thoughts about this step in the strategic thinking process.

SMART objectives and criteria

Example of SMART objective	SMART criterion
"To recommend . . .	Achievable
. . . at the June . . .	Time bound
. . . board of directors' meeting, the three . . .	Specific
. . . providers that offer the best and broadest coverage at a cost that is at least 10% less than the company's current per-employee contribution."	Realistic and measurable

Step 3: Identify Relationships, Patterns, and Trends

The capacity to understand relationships across different parts of your organization, and to spot patterns and trends in seemingly unrelated events and information, constitutes a hallmark of strategic thinking. By seeing relationships, patterns, and trends, you can generate valuable solutions to problems and reduce the amount of detail you must grapple with in order to make decisions.

Understanding how it works

Consider these examples of seeing relationships, patterns, and trends:

- **A new IT system.** By serving on a cross-functional team comprising managers from several other parts of your organization, you learn that the IT group is proposing that the company install an enterprise resource planning (ERP) system that links customer databases and other software applications throughout your company. But your group has just decided to adopt a stand-alone customer database. You realize that your group and IT will be working at cross-purposes if both plans move forward. You conclude that it would be better to hold off installing your stand-alone database until you know more about whether the ERP project will be approved.

- **Automobile manufacturing processes.** You're reading an article about a method for improving shop-floor processes in auto manufacturing. You find yourself thinking about ways to apply some of the method's principles to your own unit's operations—even though you lead a customer call center, not a manufacturing unit.

- **Defecting employees**. You work in human resources, and you notice that the employees who leave your company for jobs with other organizations increasingly tend to be those individuals who possess unique technical skills and knowledge—such as expertise with leading-edge software applications and familiarity with the latest code-writing practices. This trend prompts you to examine how your organization uses recognition and rewards to retain employees who possess unique and rare skills.

- **Customer complaints**. As you're reviewing customers' anecdotal comments on complaint forms compiled from the past year, it strikes you that many of the different comments seem related. For example, you see explicit remarks such as "Your reps don't know anything about the product you're selling." But you also see more ambiguous comments, including "Fed up with lousy treatment" and "Don't have time to keep calling." You begin to see an underlying theme related to sales representatives' competency—and devise ways to define and strengthen required competencies.

Devising solutions

Seeing patterns and trends can help you generate creative, valuable solutions to problems. For example, suppose you learned that an automaker had found a way to improve its operations—in real time, as people carried out their work. Perhaps the company stopped work processes each time a problem arose, identified the cause of the problem, and devised a trial solution that it then tested immediately on the job. In this case, you might decide to use a similar real-time experimental method to address process problems in your own unit.

For instance, perhaps your customer call center has a goal of answering calls within three rings. Yet representatives often have difficulty meeting this goal. With the auto manufacturer's method in mind, you decide to conduct a simulation: one of your employees poses as a customer and makes several phone calls to a service representative within an hour. Every time the representative can't answer the "call" within three rings, you stop the simulation and ask, "What kept you from answering on time?" You hear responses such as "I couldn't resolve the current call in time to pick up the next one" and "I didn't hear the first few rings because of a distraction in the next office."

You and your team design potential solutions to these problems, then restart the simulation to test your ideas. One thing you do is to reconfigure office space to reduce distraction. You discover that the change enables the representative to meet the goal more often. Thanks to your ability to see that a process-improvement strategy could work in two organizations as different as an auto manufacturing floor and a customer call center, you enable your group to provide better customer service.

Categorizing information

When you see patterns across supposedly unrelated information, you can more easily organize detailed information into categories—thereby reducing the number of details you need to pay attention to.

Consider a scenario about customers' comments on complaint forms. If you were unable to see patterns in the information on the forms, you might conclude that each comment represented a unique type of problem that customers were experiencing. And you'd probably feel overwhelmed by the degree of detail. Equally important, you'd find it difficult to design a solution that addresses each problem.

But what if you were able to recognize that many of the comments reflected a shared, underlying theme? You decide to contact the customers who wrote the ambiguous comments and ask for more detail. By doing this, you discover that many of these customers have experienced frustrations during their interactions with sales representatives.

You conclude that there are inadequacies in your representatives' competencies. By grouping the data into one category—employee competency—you create a more manageable degree of detail. And you focus your efforts on dealing with that one problem area.

Because the ability to see relationships, patterns, and trends helps you categorize detailed information, it enables you to process information more quickly—and therefore boosts your chances of arriving at effective solutions more speedily.

See "Tips for strengthening your ability to identify relationships, patterns, and trends" for ideas on how to enhance this important strategic thinking competency.

Use the "Worksheet for Identifying Relationships, Patterns, and Trends," located in the Tips and Tools section, to document your thoughts about this step in the process of thinking strategically.

Tips for strengthening your ability to identify relationships, patterns, and trends

- Get to know people in other functional groups by volunteering to serve on cross-functional teams or committees. Find out these groups' strategies and goals, and compare them to your group's objectives to assess whether they fit—or whether you're working at cross-purposes.

- Obtain a copy of your company's organization chart. Find out what major functions other groups in your company are responsible for and how these groups affect your group's work—and vice versa. Ask your manager or an experienced peer to help explain these connections.

- When examining large quantities of seemingly unrelated data or looking at apparently unconnected events, ask, "What seems to be the common theme underlying the different pieces of information or events? What does the data seem to be telling me?"

- Whenever you hear about or read about a good idea or practice, ask, "How might I apply this approach to my own situation? What common challenges does my group share with this seemingly different group that might mean this good idea could work for us?"

- Track changes over time for performance metrics that are important to your group. For instance, if customer loyalty, as measured by repeat purchases from key accounts, is vital to your group's performance, monitor customers' repeat purchases and watch for any signs of trouble—such as flattening or declining loyalty, or defection of key customers to a competitor.

Step 4: Get Creative

Creative thinking is the ability to generate fresh alternatives, visualize new possibilities, formulate new approaches to getting things done, and open yourself to new information that doesn't support your existing assumptions about the way people should do things at your company. When you think creatively, you create new value for your unit and company—in the form of more efficient processes, more innovative product ideas, and better ways to serve customers. In the pages that follow, you'll find ideas for getting your creative juices flowing.

Challenging your assumptions

Challenging your beliefs about how things should be done in your organization can generate valuable new ideas. To challenge assumptions, ask questions such as "Why do we believe this process should be handled only in this way? What if we did it this other way instead?"

For instance, suppose your unit has always shipped products to customers on Tuesday mornings, but this approach has led to bottlenecks in the shipping department. You ask, "Why do we ship products on Tuesday mornings only? How might customers respond if we shipped later in the day, or shipped on Wednesday?" With a little market research, you discover that customers would be equally satisfied with shipments on Tuesday evenings or Wednesday mornings. You change the shipping schedule—removing a major bottleneck in the delivery department.

Tip: Challenge current approaches to work. Consider whether you and your direct reports might work together in new, previously unimaginable ways.

Inviting provocation

Be willing to entertain ideas that strike you as provocative and even downright preposterous at first. Some of these ideas may ultimately lead to new ideas that can be turned into practical value.

For example, suppose you work for a consumer electronics company. It's Monday morning, and you're chatting with a colleague about the weekend. Your colleague happens to mention that he installed new windows in his home on Saturday. Suddenly, an image forms in your mind: a television screen with small "windows" that show what's on other channels. Though at first this idea seems strange, your company eventually develops it into an innovative feature that scores a major hit with consumers.

Tip: Model provocation. By offering playful and seemingly preposterous ideas to others, you model creative thinking. Others may emulate you—further stimulating the creative energy in your group.

Envisioning an ideal world

Sometimes imagining what might be possible in an ideal world can help you generate useful new ideas or solve a nagging problem. For instance, suppose you run a manufacturing unit, and employees are increasingly uninterested in working the weekend shifts. You conduct a brainstorming session with fellow managers to come up with solutions to the problem. Someone mentions, "We need to use better incentives with our employees. Let's pay people more to handle the weekend shifts, or withhold promotions from those who refuse to take those shifts."

While this may seem like a possible solution, you don't stop there. You ask, "In an ideal world, what would we see happen?" Someone else answers, "Well, in *my* ideal world, people would love working weekends." This comment leads you to envision a permanent Saturday/Sunday workforce that is separate from the Monday-through-Friday workforce. The idea initially seems unworkable—after all, the company has never tried this before. However, the organization agrees to test it in a pilot program—and it proves successful.

Tip: Use mind maps. On blank sheets of paper, draw pictures representing your thoughts and the ways in which they can be connected. You may generate more connections than if you merely listed ideas on a lined sheet of paper.

Gathering others' perspectives

Deliberately inviting people who work in other parts of the organization to share their views of a problem or challenge can help you see that there is more than one way to perceive a situation. For instance, imagine that you're an account manager for a product line that has experienced flat sales. You believe that the product's price may be causing the problem. You call together a group of peer managers to discuss pricing strategy. At the meeting, you present your thoughts: "As I see it, we've got three alternatives: leaving the price as is, lowering it, or raising it. Is that how you all see the situation?"

A manager from marketing responds, "You know, these aren't the only options. Have you thought about changing your promotion of the product to give it a more sophisticated image, and then using that image to justify a higher price? What about leaving the price as is and giving special discounts?" A key account manager chimes in, "You could also try lowering the price on some of the product line, or reducing it for a specific amount of time and then raising it again."

These ideas generate additional ideas from other participants in the meeting. By the end of the meeting, you've generated many more alternatives than you would have if you had stuck with your original perspective. And whenever you generate more alternatives, you stand a better chance of selecting a more effective solution to a problem than if you had considered only one or two options. Indeed, your meeting ultimately leads you to create a low-price commodity version of the product *and* a high-price premium line—both of which sell briskly.

Tip: Call on creative types. Identify the creative people
in your company. Ask them to get involved in
brainstorming sessions and other such activities if you
need help stimulating participants' creative juices.

Fostering an environment for creativity

By far the most important ingredients for creative thinking are having an open mind and not being defensive or territorial about your ideas. Create a supportive environment where people feel they can generate ideas freely, without being judged or criticized.

For example, during brainstorming sessions, allow people to blurt out as many ideas as they can generate. List all ideas without commenting on them or permitting anyone else to comment on them. Express appreciation for seemingly "wacky" ideas—the more playful and imaginative, the better. Don't worry about narrowing wide-ranging ideas down to the most practical ones until everyone has finished brainstorming.

Use toys and humor to "loosen" people up and put them in a playful mood. The more relaxed people are, the easier it is for them to envision fresh possibilities and open themselves to new ideas.

Use the "Worksheet for Thinking Creatively," located in the Tips and Tools section, to document your thoughts about this aspect of thinking strategically.

Tip: Encourage your employees to reserve time to be creative. They can block out time in their daily or weekly schedule that will not be booked with a meeting, task, or other work-related activity. Invite them to use that time to let their thoughts wander: they may well find themselves thinking of new ideas for solving old problems.

Step 5: Analyze Information

Whenever you're confronted with a complex situation on the job—whether it's making a crucial decision, managing a complex initiative, solving a problem, or improving a process—you often must wrestle with large volumes of information. How do you ensure that you've got all the right information at hand? And how do you weed out irrelevant information so you can address the situation most effectively? The following guidelines can help.

Identifying critical information you need

Before you gather information, begin by listing the critical information you need to know in order to resolve the issue facing you. One way to do this is to step away from the details of the situation and view the issue from a fresh perspective by asking questions as if you were an outsider.

For instance, suppose you run an order-fulfillment group. Recent survey results indicate that customers are not satisfied with the timeliness of their order deliveries. You believe there might be a demand for an expedited delivery service at a premium price. To explore this option, you might ask those in your unit the following questions:

- How is increasing the level of customer service a strategic goal for our unit?

- How might the overall level of customer satisfaction be improved?

- Have customers voiced a need to have products shipped faster?

- Do other companies who compete with us offer expedited delivery options?

- If we did offer an expedited delivery service, how might that have an impact on other groups in the company? For example, how quickly could the IT group add this information to the order-entry screen?

- How might faster order-fulfillment times affect inventory management?

- Has anyone in the organization rolled out a similar type of service in the last year or two? If so, what lessons can we learn from that experience?

- Does the order-fulfillment group have the capability to provide this type of service?

As you sort through the information you receive, consider the 80-20 principle, which offers helpful lessons for prioritizing information. This rule (often referred to as the Pareto principle, or the "law of the vital few") states that the relationship between input and output is rarely, if ever, balanced.

When applied to work, it means that approximately 20 percent of your activities produce 80 percent of your results. The 80-20 rule reminds you to focus on the 20 percent that really matters.

What Would YOU Do?

Dispensing Efficiency at ExcelCare?

A NDREA IS A PURCHASING MANAGER at ExcelCare, a major medical center. Top management has challenged all departments to find ways to improve efficiencies in processes, among other strategic goals. Andrea talks with peer managers in other departments to see what they're doing to meet the organization's goals. She also calls a friend, Kevin, who works in purchasing for another hospital, and asks what they're doing to achieve similar goals.

Kevin tells Andrea about a new electronic system his group has implemented to keep track of supplies inventory. Nurses and doctors needing supplies go to a vending device, punch in a few codes, and the items are dispensed. The device updates—in real time—how many of each item have been used and when. This information is synchronized with inventory records to ensure that supplies don't run low. When inventory reaches a certain level, the system sends an electronic purchase requisition to the vendor. This new system, Kevin tells Andrea, has vastly improved efficiency of the purchasing process.

Andrea calls Marcus, a colleague in IT, and asks if such a system could be implemented at ExcelCare. Marcus thinks it's conceivable. But, he warns, it would require a substantial capital investment. Andrea wonders how she should proceed from here. Should she get more information on these systems and craft a proposal advocating adoption of the system at ExcelCare? Talk with nurses and physicians at ExcelCare about how they're currently accessing supplies and whether they're experiencing any problems?

What would YOU do? The mentor will suggest a solution in *What You COULD Do.*

Identify and focus on those things that contribute to that 20 percent and you will be well on your way to analyzing information more productively and effectively.

Steering clear of irrelevant information

Don't bother considering information that's unnecessary, marginally useful, or overly time consuming to collect—even if it strikes you as interesting. Focus your information-gathering efforts on data that will help you move forward to a resolution.

For example, with the question of expedited delivery service, you might find yourself wondering how late deliveries are affecting your customers. But having this information won't help you determine whether to introduce a new service. You already know that late deliveries are bad for business. To address the issue, you need to analyze the issue from a broad perspective and understand the impact that your proposed actions might have on others.

In addition, when your information yields marginal results, try not to overanalyze small discrepancies. For example, suppose you're exploring product defects created by a piece of manufacturing equipment. In one week, the machine might generate 150 defective products. In another week, the machine might generate 160 flawed products. In all likelihood, it's not worth your time to investigate why one week's defective products are slightly higher than the previous week's. If, however, the discrepancy is greater—say 150 defective products in one week versus 450 in another—then you probably should explore the matter further.

The question to continually ask is: "Would gathering more information fundamentally change the answer that you already have?" If the answer is no, then you need to move on. If it's yes, then you need to collect more information.

Tip: Get critical. With every problem or decision you're considering, identify the most important information you have on hand and the vital data you're missing.

Crafting an information-gathering plan

Determine how, where, when, and from whom you will gather the information you need to address your issue. Conversations with people inside and outside your organization, written materials, group discussions, surveys, Internet searches, and direct observation can all be sources of information.

For instance, to determine whether to introduce an expedited delivery service, you might gather information by talking with your boss about the need to improve order-delivery times. You might also visit the various sites (warehouses, customer service centers, distribution centers) that make up your order-fulfillment system and interview personnel to find out ways to improve the process. During these visits, you could:

- Inquire about problems workers are encountering in carrying out their jobs.

- Ask about changes in their unit (such as new hires or new technologies) that may be creating difficulties.

- Ask about possible negative outcomes they might encounter if an expedited delivery service were adopted.

- Listen for possible root causes of the late-delivery problem— such as lack of awareness of expectations or inefficiencies in certain processes.

While visiting these sites, you might also take time to observe how people are carrying out their work and resolving difficulties as they arise. Again, look for possible root causes of your problem, and use your conclusions to begin thinking about solutions.

Tip: Ask the five whys. When you identify a problem, ask, "Why is this happening?" When you hear the answer, ask why again. Ask why at least five times to ensure sufficient depth of analysis.

Building on existing knowledge

Avoid reinventing the wheel. Instead, ask: "Have I or someone else in the organization faced a similar situation in the past? If so, how was it handled? What were the results? How might we fine-tune the solution to accommodate conditions that have changed since that earlier time?"

For example, ask other managers how they've handled delays in their groups' key processes. They may have developed solutions or strategies that you can adapt or apply directly to your own situation. They may also know something about certain steps in your process that can shed light on possible solutions.

Tip: Leverage insights and wisdom that others have gained by addressing issues and situations similar to the one you're currently handling.

Use the "Worksheet for Analyzing Information," located in the Tips and Tools section, to record your thoughts about this step in the strategic thinking process.

What You COULD Do.

Remember Andrea's question about what to do next regarding the electronic inventory system idea for ExcelCare?

Here's what the mentor suggests:

Andrea should talk informally with doctors and nurses (her internal customers) to learn about their needs and concerns regarding supplies. As she conducts these conversations, she may gain insights into how best to set up an electronic purchasing system. She may also think of additional ideas worthy of consideration—a range of alternatives that may boost her chances of selecting the best possible solutions to problems with managing purchasing and inventory control problems.

While an electronic inventory system sounds promising, making a proposal at this stage is premature. Andrea should first talk with all the potential stakeholders of this idea—everyone who would be affected by adoption of the new system or who would have an interest in its outcome. Only then can she learn about their needs and concerns and eventually propose a plan that best serves the entire organization.

Step 6: Prioritize Your Actions

K nowing how to prioritize your actions constitutes another aspect of applying your strategic thinking skills. In any business situation—whether it's managing a project, planning your day, making a decision, or solving a problem—you can spend your time and energy in an almost infinite number of ways. Two powerful ways to prioritize your actions are by establishing time lines and always keeping the big picture in sight.

Establishing time lines

Think about the goals you want to accomplish and the strategic initiatives you're managing. Create clear, realistic time lines for achieving these objectives. The more realistic your time line, the better your chance of avoiding the chaos and inefficient use of resources that occur when people set impossible schedules.

To establish a realistic time line for a strategic initiative:

1. **Estimate the length of time each phase will take**. Create a chart or diagram depicting the time needed for each phase. Calculate the time required to carry out the entire effort.

2. **Compare your individual and total time estimates to the time required on similar efforts that have been completed**. Do your estimates seem realistic? Do you need to add contingency time in the schedule to accommodate potential delays?

Where might it be possible to tighten up the schedule to liberate time for another phase of the initiative?

3. **Identify phases that can't be completed until other phases are complete.** These represent potential bottlenecks in the process.

4. **After making any necessary revisions to your time line, ask several colleagues or members of your team to examine the schedule and identify potential problems with it.** Also consult people who will be implementing various aspects of the initiative, as well as customers, suppliers, and other external stakeholders. They can offer additional valuable insight into potential problems with your time line.

5. **After gathering a wide range of input, develop solutions to identified problems and create a final version of your time line.**

Keeping the big picture in sight

As you consider the many different tasks you want to complete today, tomorrow, or later this week, you may well find yourself compiling a dauntingly long "to do" list. Rather than tackling the various tasks at random, picking off the easiest or quickest tasks first, or plowing through them in the order in which you've listed them, take a moment to prioritize your list items based on how well they support the big picture—your company's and unit's high-level goals.

Ask yourself, "Which of these are the most critical—that is, which will generate the most important results for my group and company? Which are more peripheral—in other words, they don't have as much bearing on my group's or company's high-priority goals? If I ran this company, which of these tasks would I pay someone to work on?"

Tip: Schedule high-priority work. Block out time in your calendar for strategically important activities, so your schedule doesn't fill up with peripheral tasks and meetings.

Remember that some tasks may be urgent but not important in the big scheme of things. For instance, a report may be due by the end of the day (urgent), but completing it on time may contribute little or nothing to your group's high-level goals (not important). If you give in to completing urgent but not important tasks, you risk neglecting more strategically valuable actions.

By identifying high-priority actions, you can more easily figure out how to use your time and which tasks to focus on in what sequence. You can divide your workload into parts and determine which parts should be done today, tomorrow, next week, and next month. You can also more readily identify which less strategically important actions can be delegated to members of your team—or even be left undone.

Use the "Worksheet for Prioritizing Your Actions," located in the Tips and Tools section, to generate some thoughts about this step in thinking strategically.

Step 7: Make Trade-Offs

Strategic thinking also includes assessing the trade-offs involved in selecting a particular course of action—and selecting the most appropriate trade-off. Most decisions involve a trade-off. For example, suppose you oversee a product development group and your team is charged with creating a new product. The director of sales asks if you can release the product four weeks ahead of schedule to satisfy a major customer. You know this decision will require people in other groups—marketing, manufacturing, customer service, fulfillment, and so forth—to expedite their work for an earlier delivery date. You also know that the quality of the product could be jeopardized. You decide to risk losing the sale to the major customer and release the product on schedule as originally planned.

As this example suggests, making trade-offs involves setting priorities, identifying alternatives, understanding the impact of your actions, and clarifying what you will strive to accomplish through a particular course of action—as well as what you won't seek to attain. The following practices can you help you navigate through this difficult terrain.

Assessing the pros and cons of a proposed course of action

Whenever you consider a potential course of action—a new strategy for your group, a new product feature, an initiative to improve a business process—ask yourself what advantages and disadvantages

Pros and cons of new product feature

Advantages	Disadvantages
Lets us charge a higher price	Might cannibalize sales of previous product version
Might attract new customer segments	Could be perceived as unnecessary or annoying by consumers
Could improve brand awareness: our company is on the leading edge of technology	Would require expensive redesign of base product

might be associated with that course of action. The table, "Pros and cons of new product feature," gives an example of how one manager conducted this assessment.

You are unlikely to be able to do it all—develop a new product feature that avoids expensive redesign, that doesn't threaten sales of earlier product versions, that can be sold at a sufficiently high price, and so forth. Thus, you need to make trade-offs.

How to do so? Consider your company's and unit's strategic goals. Do these goals emphasize reducing costs? Improving brand awareness? Simplifying product-development processes? Your answers can help guide your decisions about what's okay to trade off—and what isn't.

Comparing short- and long-term outcomes

In considering a course of action, think through the potential short- and long-term impacts of your choice. For example, suppose you're wondering whether to cut prices on a product line that has experienced declining sales. You realize that cutting prices may boost sales this month or this year. But in the long run, this move could hurt sales. How? Perhaps consumers would come to expect deep discounts on your company's offerings. Thus, they would hold off purchasing your products until you provide another discount. These delays could reduce sales over the long term. However, if boosting sales immediately is a high priority in your company, you may decide to trade off future sales increases for current sales increases.

By sharpening your awareness of the possible short- and long-term consequences of your choices, you can make smarter trade-offs. "Steps for balancing short-term requirements with long-term goals" provides additional guidance for this aspect of making trade-offs.

Steps for balancing short-term requirements with long-term goals

1. **Meet with your boss to determine how much time you and your team should be allocating toward short-term issues versus long-term goals.**
2. **Review the work that you and your team have done in the past month to determine what has been accomplished on both short- and long-term issues.** If the balance is not right according to your group's priorities, set new guidelines for how you and your team spend your time.
3. **Keep an ongoing log to determine how you and your team are spending your time.**

4. **Every two weeks, evaluate whether you and your team are giving the proper time and attention to short-term requirements and long-term goals.** Again, if the balance is not right according to your group's priorities, readjust your focus appropriately.

5. **When you face competing priorities, determine which are the most important and make those your first priority.** When an urgent matter arises, determine how it fits into your daily plan (is it urgent and important, or simply urgent?) and act accordingly.

6. **Ask your team how it can make progress on long-term issues while addressing short-term needs.** For example, a goal may be to develop a line of products for a new market. Ask the team to figure out how to make progress on that goal while also developing products for existing markets.

Balancing unit and company needs

Some decisions involve trade-offs between your department or group and the company overall. To illustrate, suppose you lead a sales group whose representatives have won numerous new accounts by promising customers early delivery dates on a new product. That's great for your group. However, it puts a burden on the product development, manufacturing, order processing, and customer service departments—all of which must accelerate their processes in order to meet the promises the sales reps have made.

This situation may lead to several possible outcomes:

- Your group's actions may have a negative impact on other groups. For example, forcing product development to release a product early may jeopardize the quality of the product. This in turn, might affect the product development unit's strategy of trying to raise the quality standard of all products.

- In the end, your group's actions could thus eventually hurt relationships with other groups and with long-standing, existing customers.

In this case, you might need to consider whether to trade off some new sales in return for smoother operation of the rest of your company's functions, so your organization can serve *all* its customers, not just the newest ones.

Tip: Ask whether a decision that could help your group vastly improve its performance might pose such serious problems for other parts of your organization that the gains for your group might not be worth the price other groups will pay.

Learning to say no

At times, making a trade-off requires nothing more than specifying what you *won't* do—and not bothering with articulating what you *will* do. Setting boundaries like this is tremendously valuable because it helps you avoid wasting time on projects or initiatives that you don't support or that will be shut down later.

For example, suppose your group is evaluating the possibility of creating tiered versions of a product—high-end, mid-market, low-end. You've made a strong argument against introducing a low-end product: "It'll hurt our brand image, and it will generate lower profits for us." In this case, you might indicate your trade-off decision by saying something like, "I don't know what a high-end version of the product would look like. But I do know that we won't do a low-end version."

By defining the trade-off in this way, you help your group to focus on the acceptable courses of action—and to develop or maintain strategies for ensuring success.

Tip: Think *will* and *won't*. In making a complex decision or considering an important course of action, identify what you will and won't do.

Use the "Worksheet for Making Trade-Offs," located in the Tips and Tools section, to document your thoughts about this step in the strategic thinking process.

Tips and Tools

Tools for Thinking Strategically

Worksheet for Seeing the Big Picture

Use this tool to gain a sense of the "business ecosystem" in which you operate. Seeing the big picture can help you set the stage for thinking strategically about your work.

Part I: Your company and unit

1. What is your company's competitive strategy? If you don't know, what steps might you take to find out? *Consider asking your boss and peer managers, as well as examining company documents and executive communications.*

2. What are your unit's strategic objectives? How do those objectives relate to the corporate strategy? *For example, if you work in a product development unit, has your unit defined a strategy stipulating development of new product lines to support a high-level strategy focused on innovation?*

3. What actions, plans, and decisions might enable your group to help support your unit's and company's strategies? *Consider potential process improvements, better management of costs, new revenue opportunities, and other potentially valuable courses of action.*

Part II: Your customers, competitors, and industry

4. Who are your company's customers? *Consider various customer segments as well as any internal customers your group may serve if you work in a support function.*

5. What needs and preferences does your organization currently fulfill for its customers? *What unique forms of value does your company offer its customers?*

6. How might your customers' needs and preferences evolve in the future? *Do you anticipate demand for faster service, higher-quality products, more affordable offerings?*

7. What could your group do to help your company fulfill customers' changing requirements? *Consider process improvements, product ideas, and other means of enhancing the value your organization provides customers.*

8. With what organizations does your company compete? *Ask your boss, peer managers, and business acquaintances for input.*

9. What industry trends might have important implications for your company's business? *Consult business publications and talk with other informed professionals to assess these trends.*

10. How might your group take advantage of opportunities offered by emerging industry trends or stave off threats posed by such trends? *Cite as many examples as you can.*

Part III: Your boss, peers, and employees

11. Think of a decision you're weighing or a course of action you're considering. *Write it below.*

12. Who are all the stakeholders in this decision? *List everyone who would be affected by or have an interest in the outcome of the decision. Be sure to consider your boss, any peer managers, and employees.*

13. How will you learn about the potential impact of your decision on your various stakeholders in different parts of your organization? *List the questions you will want to ask your stakeholders.*

14. If you've consulted stakeholders about their concerns regarding your decision or proposed course of action, have you identified any underlying issues that cross multiple groups of stakeholders? If so, what are they? *Common shared concerns may include cost, time, workload, and so forth.*

15. How might you shape your decision or proposed course of action so as to address stakeholder concerns you've identified? *For example, would a pilot project help ease worries about the expense of a new initiative?*

Worksheet for Clarifying Strategic Objectives

Use this tool to articulate your group's strategic goals and aims, and to clarify what you hope to achieve through strategic thinking. Clarifying objectives enables you to set the stage for thinking strategically about your work.

1. What strategic objectives has your boss defined for you and your group? *List them below.*

2. If some or all of the objectives your boss has defined are vague or general, how might you gain further clarity and specificity? *For example, if your boss has told you "We need to be more innovative," you might ask, "Where should we focus our innovation efforts—on products? Processes? Services?"*

3. What ideas for strategic objectives might you add to those mandated by your boss? *Consider goals your group could aim for in order to make the best possible contribution to your company in the coming years.*

4. What strategic initiatives have you recently been charged with leading? *Strategic initiatives are projects—such as installing a customer relationship management (CRM) system, or enhancing quality-control processes—designed specifically to help carry out a company's or unit's strategy.*

5. What is the strategic priority that each of the initiatives you're leading is intended to serve? *For instance, is the new CRM system you're helping to research designed to enable your company to identify new customer segments?*

6. How might you ensure that your strategic initiatives' objectives remain clearly focused on the company or unit priorities they are intended to serve? *Often, initiative stakeholders have different goals in mind for a particular project—which can lead to chaos and allocation of resources away from strategic priorities.*

7. Are there alternative projects that merit consideration in addition to the strategic initiatives currently on your plate? *How do the various alternatives compare in terms of cost, feasibility, and other criteria?*

8. For each strategic initiative you're working on, write the project's objective below. *Ensure that each objective is SMART: specific, measurable, achievable, realistic, and time bound.*

Worksheet for Identifying Relationships, Patterns, and Trends

Use this tool to understand relationships, patterns, and trends in seemingly unrelated events and information. This strategic thinking ability can help you generate valuable solutions to problems and organize details into manageable levels.

1. Think of a problem you're experiencing in your group or a difficult decision you're facing. *Examples might include increased defection of talented employees, inefficiencies in a particular process, and so forth.*

2. What ideas have you read or heard about that you might borrow from to address your own situation? *Consider practices applied in other companies or industries—even if those settings differ markedly from your own.*

3. What changes over time seem to be occurring regarding the issue you're dealing with? *For example, is turnover in your group increasing at a steady pace? Rising and then falling? Increasing and then flattening out?*

4. What changes in other parts of your organization might be related to your issue? *For instance, has the company invested less in professional development programs recently? Might that change correspond with increased turnover rates in your group?*

5. What might you do to gain a broader perspective on your issue? *Could you participate in more cross-functional task forces to learn more about how changes in different parts of the company affect various units and groups?*

6. If you're evaluating a large amount of data while addressing your issue, how might you organize the data into a more manageable form? *Look for common themes underlying different pieces of information or events.*

Worksheet for Thinking Creatively

Use this tool to strengthen your creative thinking ability—an important component of strategic thinking.

1. Think of a problem you're trying to solve or a course of action you're considering. Write it below. *For example, perhaps you want to find ways to generate ideas for improving faulty customer service.*

2. What assumptions do you and your group hold regarding the issue at hand? *Do you assume, for instance, that customers must receive their orders within two days or they'll defect to a competitor?*

3. What questions might you ask to challenge these assumptions? *Could you ask, "Why do we believe this about our customers? What if we delivered orders in three or four days?"*

4. How might you stimulate creative brainstorming of ideas within your group? *Consider challenging yourself and your employees to dream up the most preposterous ideas possible—without judging one another's ideas.*

5. In your view and in the opinion of your direct reports, what would resolution of your issue look like in an ideal world? *For instance, perhaps in your vision of a perfect world, customers would care only about how easy it is to open your product's packaging and use the contents—not about when they take delivery of the order.*

6. How might you gather the broadest possible perspective on your issue? *Could you assemble a one-time cross-functional team comprising managers from other units who can offer ideas for addressing your issue? Are there individuals outside your organization—customers or suppliers—who could provide additional valuable ideas?*

7. What steps could you take to create a playful mood in which you and your group can stimulate your creative thinking? *Would toys, food, or improvisational exercises help loosen everyone up?*

Worksheet for Analyzing Information

Use this tool to strengthen your ability to analyze information—another important strategic thinking skill.

1. Consider a difficult situation, an important decision, or a pressing problem you're facing in your group. Write it below. *Examples might include recurring customer complaints, declining employee performance, flattening sales, and so forth.*

2. What critical information do you need to know in order to resolve your issue? *List as many questions as you can think of that may generate the information you need—and think of the issue from a broad organizational perspective. For example, if your issue involves improving customer call center service, you might ask questions such as, "How would improving this service support our unit's strategic goals? Do other companies provide better service? If so, in what respects? How might improving our service affect other parts of our organization, as well as processes related to our call center's work? Do we have the ability to make the desired improvements?"*

3. What information do you already have regarding your issue? *By listing this information here, you can more easily focus on gathering the needed data you've listed in step 2.*

4. Whom might you contact to gather the needed information you listed in step 2? *Will you talk with your boss? Call center employees? Customers? Competitors? Suppliers?*

5. How will you gather the information you need? *Will you visit call center sites to observe workers in action? Act as a "mystery customer" and phone a center yourself to assess the quality of the service? Phone contacts and ask for their ideas about what may be causing the problem?*

6. How might you build on existing knowledge to address your issue? *Consider whether you or someone else in your organization has dealt successfully with a similar situation before. If so, how might you adapt proven solutions to your current problem?*

Worksheet for Prioritizing Your Actions

Use this tool to prioritize your actions while planning management of a strategic initiative and organizing a typical work day.

Part I: Planning a strategic initiative

1. Consider a strategic initiative you've been charged with leading. Write it below. *Examples might include setting up a new order-fulfillment system, installing a new employee database, and so forth.*

2. What phases will your initiative consist of? *For example, installing a new database might involve researching off-the-shelf applications, defining the structure of the database contents, testing early versions, and so forth.*

3. How much time do you anticipate needing to complete each phase of the initiative? The total initiative? *Compare your estimates to times required on similar projects that have been completed.*

4. Where in your schedule are delays most likely, and how will you handle them? *Consider building more time into these phases of the initiative.*

5. Which initiative tasks depend on completion of other tasks? *These represent potential bottlenecks, and merit extra attention during execution of the initiative.*

6. How will you gather feedback on your proposed timeline so as to create a final, realistic version? *Consider asking colleagues, employees, people who will be implementing parts of the initiative, and any other stakeholders to identify potential problems with your working time line.*

Part II: Organizing a work day

7. The next time you come to work on a Monday morning, list all the things you want to accomplish that day. *List tasks as they come to mind, without trying to organize them just yet.*

8. Review your list. Which items are the most critical? *Critical items are those that generate the most valuable results for your group and company when completed.*

9. Which items on your list are peripheral? *Peripheral items have little or no bearing on your group's or company's high-priority objectives.*

10. Which items are urgent but not important? *Some tasks are time sensitive but have little strategic value.*

11. How will you schedule the critical tasks on your list to ensure that they're completed effectively and on time? *Divide work into parts, if necessary, to help you determine which tasks to focus on in which sequence. Consider what parts of the work must be done today, tomorrow, next week, next month, and so forth.*

12. Which items on your list can be delegated to members of your team? Which can be left undone with no harmful impact on your group or company? *Knowing when to delegate and when to ignore strategically irrelevant tasks can help you focus further on critical items on your list.*

Worksheet for Making Trade-Offs

Use this tool to make smart trade-offs while grappling with a difficult decision or problem.

1. Identify an important decision or problem you're facing. *For example, a key design expert on a new product has fallen behind schedule in handling his part of the project, and you must decide whether to delay launch of the product so as to incorporate his expertise or go ahead without it.*

2. What are your choices regarding the issue you're facing? *For instance, you could delay the product launch, borrow an existing design and launch the product on time, find another skilled designer who can step in immediately and take over that part of the project, and so forth.*

3. What are the pros and cons of each of the choices you listed in step 2? *For example, delaying the product launch would ensure that the product embodied cutting-edge design, but it would risk losing sales to eager customers who expect to purchase the new offering by the original promised date.*

4. How might knowledge of your company's or unit's strategic goals inform your decision? *If your company's strategy emphasizes increasing sales revenues, you might decide to keep the product on schedule—and trade off design innovation for sales.*

5. What are the potential short- and long-term ramifications of your choices? *Launching the product on schedule but with a less-than-stellar design might generate needed sales in the short run but reduce sales in the long run if customers decide that the product is mediocre.*

6. What cross-functional considerations should you take into account while making your decision? *For instance, delaying launch of the product—even if it's the right thing to do overall—could overburden the sales group if they have already committed their energy to introducing other products during the time when you now want to launch your new product.*

7. Taking all of your above responses into account—pros and cons of alternatives, your company's and unit's strategic goals, short- and long-term consequences of your choices, and cross-functional considerations—what trade-off seems most appropriate to make in this situation? *Write your decision, and explain your rationale.*

Strategic Thinking Self-Assessment

Part I: Assessment

Use this tool to assess your strategic thinking abilities. For each statement below, indicate how accurately the statement describes you. "1" indicates "Rarely," "5" indicates "Usually." Be sure to answer based on your actual behavior in real workplace situations. That way, you'll have the most accurate assessment of your skills.

Statement	Rating				
	Rarely				Usually
	1	2	3	4	5
1. I ask questions about what's going on in my unit, company, industry, and wider business environment.					
2. I am able to adapt approaches and shift ideas when new information suggests the need to do so.					
3. I look for opportunities today that might generate valuable results tomorrow.					
4. I view challenges as opportunities.					
5. I welcome new ideas and opinions—even if they seem strange at first.					
6. I take criticism well by not reacting in a defensive manner.					
7. I work to broaden my knowledge, experience, and skill set.					
8. I seek other people's opinions.					
9. I anticipate how my actions will affect others around me.					
10. I question my own long-standing assumptions and encourage others to question theirs.					
11. I understand the forces influencing my group's performance.					
12. I know who my company's customers are and what they value.					
13. I know who my company's competitors are and what makes us different from them.					

14. I stay up to date on important trends affecting my company's industry and my group's operations.	
15. I objectively analyze situations.	
16. I evaluate the pros, cons, and implications of different courses of action.	
17. I grasp abstract ideas and put the "pieces" together to form a coherent picture.	
18. I generate a wide variety of options, visualize new possibilities, and formulate fresh approaches.	
19. I see patterns across unrelated events and information.	
20. I can sift out irrelevant from relevant information while deciding how to solve a problem or handle a challenge.	
21. I can often visualize new possibilities that others have trouble seeing.	
22. I try to generate multiple alternative courses of action while making important decisions.	
23. I compare the potential short- and long-term consequences of actions I'm considering.	
24. I consider whether improvements I'm making to my own group's operations may create problems for people in other parts of my organization.	
25. I stay focused on my objectives while handling multiple demands and competing priorities.	
Total score *(Calculate your score by adding up the numbers for each of your responses.)*	

Part II: Scoring	
Use the following table to interpret your score.	
104–125	**Exceptional:** You're a talented strategic thinker who possesses many of the traits, behaviors, attitudes, and cognitive capacities that are necessary for thinking strategically.
78–103	**Superior:** You're a highly effective strategic thinker in many areas but would benefit from refining some of your skills.
51–77	**Adequate:** You know and practice many of the basics of strategic thinking. However, you can increase your success by further extending your skills.
25–50	**Deficient:** You'll need to work broadly on your strategic thinking skills so that you can learn how to analyze opportunities and problems from a broad perspective and understand an action's potential impact on others.

Test Yourself

This section offers ten multiple-choice questions to help you identify your baseline knowledge of the essentials of thinking strategically.

Answers to the questions are given at the end of the test.

1. What is strategic thinking?

   a. Analyzing opportunities and problems from a broad perspective and understanding your actions' potential impacts on others.

   b. Developing plans for persuading your supervisor, peer managers, employees, or customers to adopt your proposed course of action.

   c. Identifying the root causes of problems without allowing emotions to dominate or confuse your thinking process.

2. Which of the following is a personal trait that is characteristic of strategic thinkers?

   a. Keeping an eye on competitors' actions and plans.

   b. Viewing challenges as opportunities.

   c. Evaluating the pros and cons of alternative courses of action.

3. What are the two phases of the strategic thinking process?

   a. Seeing the big picture and thinking creatively.

   b. Prioritizing your actions and analyzing information.

   c. Setting the stage and applying your skills.

4. How do strategic thinkers continually improve their view of the larger "business ecosystem" in which they operate?

   a. They analyze the impact of their company's products and services on high-level, emerging developments such as the accelerating globalization of business and organizations' increasing emphasis on improving customer service.

   b. They understand their company's and unit's strategies; consider what's going on with customers, competitors, and their industry; and take into account how their actions might affect others in their organization.

   c. They stay on top of important trends in the industry in which their company competes—such as changes in governmental policy, technological advances, availability and quality of natural resources, and demographic shifts.

5. Your boss has just defined an urgent strategic objective for you: "Enhance quality to improve company performance." As a strategic thinker, how might you best respond to your boss's mandate initially?

   a. Gain insights from managers who are working in other functions about how the company has been performing and what may be contributing to performance problems.

b. Move immediately to reduce errors, improve accuracy, and incorporate cutting-edge innovation into every process for which your group is responsible.

c. Ask your boss clarifying questions, such as "What do you mean by 'enhance quality'?" and "Where should we focus our quality-enhancement efforts?"

6. Identifying relationships, patterns, and trends is an important strategic thinking skill. Which of the following is an example of this skill in action?

a. At a conference, you hear a presenter describe a new process-improvement approach being used in a different industry. You consider adapting that process in your own company.

b. While attempting to solve a recurring problem in your group, you invite your direct reports to challenge their assumptions about how work should be done in your organization.

c. To carry out a strategic mandate to improve order fulfillment for customers, you list all the critical data you need to know in order to achieve this important objective.

7. Creative thinking constitutes an important strategic thinking skill. Which of the following is a valuable outcome of creative thinking?

a. An effective plan for gathering information you need to solve a pressing business problem.

b. Awareness of underlying common themes in a wide range of data you're evaluating.

c. An open attitude toward seemingly bizarre ideas that your company hasn't considered before.

8. Analyzing information is another key strategic thinking skill. Which of the following is an example of how you might apply this skill?

a. Borrow from previously developed solutions that proved useful for addressing problems such as one you're currently dealing with.

b. Gather all information directly and indirectly related to a current challenge, so you can compile the most comprehensive data possible.

c. Concentrate your information analysis on what's going on in your immediate group, since you're most familiar with that source of data.

9. How might a strategic thinker best approach accomplishing a long list of "to do's" facing him or her at the start of a workday?

a. Tackle the easiest items first so as to get rid of distractions and then focus more sharply on the most important activities and tasks.

b. Identify and schedule the most critical items on the list first, while delegating or leaving undone any peripheral items.

c. Address all urgent responsibilities immediately, since these constitute the most important items on the list.

10. Knowing how to make smart trade-offs is a vital strategic thinking skill. Which of the following approaches can help you apply this skill?

a. Weighing the short- and long-term consequences of a proposed course of action.

b. Identifying the full range of possible advantages offered by a decision you advocate.

c. Optimizing your group's performance to improve company performance overall.

Answers to test questions

1, a. Because you work in a particular part of your organization, you have only so much information at hand to address difficult problems and make important decisions. Strategic thinking helps you overcome these limitations. How? It enables you to view workplace challenges from a broad perspective and anticipate your decisions' possible impact on other individuals and parts of your organization. As a result, you make smarter choices and select the most appropriate courses of action to generate valuable results for your organization.

2, b. In addition to a positive outlook that enables them to view challenges as opportunities, strategic thinkers demonstrate other characteristic personal traits—such as curiosity about their company and industry, flexibility in the face of new information, a focus on the future, and a breadth of knowledge and experience.

3, c. In phase 1 of the strategic thinking process, setting the stage, you seek to understand the broader business environment in which you operate and to clarify your strategic objectives. In phase 2, you apply your strategic thinking skills—which include identifying relationships, patterns, and trends; thinking creatively; analyzing information; prioritizing your actions; and making trade-offs.

4, b. Improving your view of the larger "business ecosystem" means constantly monitoring what's going on both inside and outside your organization—and using your awareness to make smart on-the-job choices that ensure your company's best possible future. Familiarizing yourself with company- and unit-level strategy; understanding changes in customers, competitors, and your industry; and anticipating how your choices may have an impact on people and processes in other parts of your organization all help you gain the broad perspective you need to make savvy business decisions.

5, c. When your boss defines strategic objectives for you, it's important to ensure that you understand those objectives in the most specific terms possible. Asking clarifying questions can help you avoid misunderstandings about goals, specify areas where you should invest your effort and time, and anticipate possible impacts of any changes on other parts of the organization. In addition to asking their boss clarifying questions, strategic thinkers also offer ideas for additional objectives that may help their group support company-level strategies.

6, a. Spotting opportunities to leverage best practices from industries very different from yours is an example of the ability to identify relationships, patterns, and trends—particularly in seemingly unrelated arenas. Application of this strategic thinking skill also enables you to understand relationships across different parts of your organization, interpret changes across time in important performance metrics (such as employee turnover or revenues), and organize seemingly disparate information into more manageable categories.

7, c. Generating fresh alternatives (even if they seem initially preposterous), visualizing new possibilities, formulating new approaches to getting things done, and opening yourself to new information that doesn't support your existing assumptions are all hallmarks of creative thinking. By enabling you to generate more alternatives rather than limiting your choices to just the first one or two that come to mind, creative thinking boosts your chances of ultimately selecting the best possible course of action.

8, a. Building on existing knowledge is one valuable way to apply your skill at analyzing information. By adapting proved solutions, you save time and help spread wisdom gained in other parts of your organization. Other ways to apply this skill include determining the critical information you need to address the issue at hand, as well as developing and implementing an effective information-gathering plan.

9, b. By prioritizing your actions in this way, you keep your eye on the big picture—a key element of strategic thinking.

All managers are busy and have many responsibilities. Part of being a strategic thinker is knowing how to identify and prioritize the critical tasks on your long list of "to do's"—those activities that will generate the most valuable results for your group and company. More peripheral items can be postponed, delegated, or even left undone if necessary, so you can focus your time and energy on strategically relevant activities.

10, a. Some trade-offs involve sacrificing short-term gains in order to achieve important long-term gains, or vice versa. Thus, weighing the possible short- and long-term consequences of a proposed course of action, and considering how each of those consequences relates to your company's strategic goals, can help you make smart trade-offs. Other approaches to making wise trade-offs include assessing the pros and cons of alternative courses of action, considering whether actions that benefit your group will also benefit the rest of your organization, and specifying what you won't do to resolve a problem or achieve a goal.

To Learn More

Articles

Christensen, Clayton M. "Making Strategy: Learning by Doing." *Harvard Business Review*, November 1997.

> Companies find it difficult to change strategy for many reasons, but one stands out: strategic thinking is not a core managerial competence at most companies. Managers are unable to develop competence in strategic thinking because they do it so rarely. Harvard Business School Professor Clayton Christensen helps managers develop a creative strategy and a proficiency in strategic decision making. This article presents a three-stage method executives can use to conceive and implement a creative and coherent strategy themselves. The three-step process forces managers to dig deep in order to understand the forces affecting their business. This method is a useful tool for managers because it helps them link strategic thinking with operational planning: two processes that are often separate but are more effective when connected.

Collis, David J., and Michael G. Rukstad, "Can You Say What Your Strategy Is?" *Harvard Business Review*, April 2008.

Can you summarize your company's strategy in 35 words or less? Would your colleagues express it the same way? Very few executives can honestly say yes to those simple questions. The thing is, companies with a clear, concise strategy statement—one that employees can easily internalize and use as a guiding light—often turn out to be industry stars. In this article, Harvard Business School's Collis and Rukstad provide a practical guide for crafting an effective strategy statement and include an in-depth example of how the St. Louis–based brokerage firm Edward Jones developed one that has generated success.

Harvard Business School Publishing. "Essentials: The Building Blocks of Strategy." *Harvard Management Update*, January 2006.

If you haven't had a great deal of experience with formulating a strategy for your business or unit, you're in good company. It's not an everyday activity. This article walks you through the steps you need to take: (1) scan the outer environment for threats and opportunities; (2) look inside at resources, capabilities, and practices; (3) consider how you will address threats and opportunities you've identified; (4) build a good "fit" among strategy-supporting activities; and (5) create alignment between the people and the activities of the organization and its strategy. And remember—no strategy lasts forever, so learn to use these steps again and again to keep your strategy responsive to the ever-changing business environment. (Note: This article is adapted from *Manager's Toolkit*, published by Harvard Business School Press in 2004.)

Slywotzky, Adrian J., and John Drzik. "Countering the Biggest Risk of All." *Harvard Business Review* OnPoint Enhanced Edition, April 2005.

Slywotzky and Drzik provide examples of how managers working in a wide variety of organizations apply the strategic thinking skill of seeing the big picture. In particular, the authors show how to assess the implications of important "business ecosystem" developments—such as technology shifts, the emergence of new competitors, industrywide commoditization of products and erosion of profit margins, changes in customer priorities, and maturation of markets. Slywotzky and Drzik then offer strategies for countering such developments, showing how particular organizations have used these strategies successfully.

Spear, Steven J. "Fixing Health Care from the Inside, Today." *Harvard Business Review* OnPoint Enhanced Edition, September 2005.

Spear provides a case study of strategic thinking in action—particularly the ability to identify relationships, patterns, and trends. The author describes how health care professionals at several hospitals applied a strategy used by a major automobile manufacturer to identify and correct process problems. Though the two industries are very different, health care practitioners realized that the automobile manufacturer's process-improvement approach could help them reduce errors in patient care, save lives, and cut costs.

Stalk Jr., George. "Curveball: Strategies to Fool the Competition." *Harvard Business Review* OnPoint Enhanced Edition, September 2006.

In this follow-up piece to his article "Hardball: Five Killer Strategies for Trouncing the Competition" (HBR, April 2004), George Stalk Jr. of the Boston Consulting Group offers another approach for prevailing over rivals. Strategic hardball is about playing rough and tough with competitors; strategic curveball is about outfoxing them. It involves getting rivals to do something dumb that they otherwise wouldn't (that is, swing at a pitch that appears to be in the strike zone but isn't) or not do something smart that they otherwise would (that is, fail to swing at a pitch that's in the strike zone but appears not to be). Stalk describes four types of curveball and provides extended examples of curveball strategies in action at companies such as the industrial-cleaning chemical supplier Ecolab and the Australian airline Jetstar.

Books

Langdon, Bruce, Andy Langdon, and Ken Langdon. *Strategic Thinking*. The DK Essential Managers Series. New York: Dorling Kindersley, 2000.

This concise volume provides tips for applying your strategic thinking skills—including understanding your customers and competitors, making trade-offs between the short and long term, clarifying your strategic objectives, assessing the pros and cons of alternative courses of action, and much more. Tables, graphics, and case studies all serve to illustrate key points and summarize important information.

De Bono, Edward. *Six Thinking Hats*. Boston: Little, Brown, 1985.

De Bono, a leading international authority in the teaching of thinking as a skill, provides easy-to-follow guidelines for applying the many skills that constitute strategic thinking. Any manager, he maintains, can shift from skill to skill by "putting on" the appropriate "thinking hat." For example, donning the "white hat" enables you to evaluate facts, figures, and objective information, while shifting to the "green hat" helps you spark your creative thinking. A wealth of examples from a broad range of organizations helps to illustrate the six thinking skills De Bono presents.

Kim, W. Chan, and Renée Mauborgne. *Blue Ocean Strategy: How to Create Uncontested Market Space and Make the Competition Irrelevant.* Boston: Harvard Business School Press, 2004.

Since the dawn of the industrial age, companies have engaged in head-to-head competition in search of sustained, profitable growth. They have fought for competitive advantage, battled over market share, and struggled for differentiation. Yet, these hallmarks of competitive strategy are not the way to create profitable growth in the future. In a book that challenges everything you thought you knew about the requirements for strategic success, W. Chan Kim and Renée Mauborgne argue that cutthroat competition results in nothing but a bloody red ocean of rivals fighting over a shrinking profit pool. Based on a study of a hundred fifty strategic moves spanning more than a hundred years and thirty industries, the authors argue that lasting success comes not from battling competitors, but from creating "blue oceans"—untapped new market spaces ripe for growth. Such strategic moves—which the authors call "value innovation"—create powerful leaps in value that often render rivals obsolete for more than a decade. *Blue Ocean Strategy* presents a systematic approach to making the competition irrelevant and outlines principles and tools any company can use to create and capture blue oceans. A landmark work that upends traditional thinking about strategy, this book charts a bold new path to winning the future.

Strategy: Create and Implement the Best Strategy for Your Business. Harvard Business Essentials Series. Boston: Harvard Business School Press, 2005.

This book helps you focus on the strategic thinking skill of seeing the big picture—in particular, understanding your company's and unit's strategies and knowing how to help execute them. The author explains how to assess your company's and unit's strengths, weaknesses, opportunities, and threats (a SWOT analysis); describes common competitive strategies and strategic moves used in the business world; and explains how to develop action plans for implementing strategy. Additional chapters provide guidelines for keeping your implementation plan on course, motivating your people to execute strategy, and continually testing and revising your strategy as needed.

eLearning

Harvard Business School Publishing. *Case in Point.* Boston: Harvard Business School Publishing, 2004.

Case in Point is a flexible set of online cases, designed to help prepare middle- and senior-level managers for a variety of leadership challenges. These short, reality-based scenarios provide sophisticated content to create a focused view into the realities of the life of a leader. Your managers will experience: Aligning Strategy, Removing Implementation Barriers, Overseeing Change, Anticipating Risk, Ethical Decisions, Building a Business Case, Cultivating Customer Loyalty, Emotional Intelligence, Developing a Global Perspective, Fostering Innovation, Defining Problems, Selecting Solutions, Managing Difficult Interactions, The Coach's Role, Delegating for Growth, Managing Creativity, Influencing Others, Managing Performance, Providing Feedback, and Retaining Talent.

Sources for Thinking Strategically

The following sources aided in development of this book:

De Bono, Edward. *Six Thinking Hats*. Boston: Little, Brown and Company, 1985.

Gavetti, Giovanni, and Jan W. Rivkin. "How Strategists Really Think: Tapping the Power of Analogy." *Harvard Business Review* OnPoint Enhanced Edition. April 2005.

Johnson, Lauren Keller. "Debriefing Paul Nutt: Increase the Odds of Being Right." *Harvard Management Update*, June 2005.

Slywotzky, Adrian J., and John Drzik. "Countering the Biggest Risk of All." *Harvard Business Review* OnPoint Enhanced Edition. April 2005.

Spear, Steven J. "Fixing Health Care from the Inside, Today." *Harvard Business Review* OnPoint Enhanced Edition. April 2006.

"Strategic Thinking," white paper, Interaction Associates, April 2005.

Successful Manager's Handbook: Development Suggestions for Today's Managers. 2nd ed. Minneapolis: Personnel Decisions International, 1992.

Successful Manager's Handbook: Develop Yourself, Coach Others. 7th ed. Minneapolis: Personnel Decisions International, 2004.

Notes

Notes

Notes

Notes

Notes

Notes

Notes

Notes

Notes

How to Order

Harvard Business School Press publications are available world-wide from your local bookseller or online retailer.

You can also call:
1-800-668-6780

Our product consultants are available to help you 8:00 a.m.–6:00 p.m., Monday–Friday, Eastern Time. Outside the U.S. and Canada, call: 617-783-7450.

Please call about special discounts for quantities greater than ten.

You can order online at:
www.HBSPress.org